Questions, Answers & Explanations

EASA PPL Revision Papers

Human Performance & Limitations

Written and illustrated by
Helena B A Hughes

POOLEY'S
Air Pilot Publishing

STOP PRESS – New UK CAA PPL e-Exams - The UK CAA are introducing new PPL e-Exams from October 2020. Rather than using paper exam sets, all the exams will now be taken online under controlled conditions. They will, however, still be taken at your flying school and under the supervision of an approved individual. Please note that the syllabus has not changed. By reading the Air Pilots Manuals and other reading materials mentioned in the books, and by testing yourself with the following test papers, you will be ready to undertake these new exams. The CAA has issued guidance for students taking these exams and this can be found by searching online for CAP1903G.

Copyright © 2020 Pooleys Flight Equipment Limited.
Some images copyright © 2020 Pooleys Air Pilot Publishing Ltd.

EASA Private Pilot Licence Aeroplane & Helicopter Questions, Answers & Explanations – Human Performance & Limitations

ISBN 978-1-84336-205-0

First Edition published February 2014
Revised May 2014
Reprint September 2015
Reprint February 2016
Reprint January 2017
Revised Edition July 2017
Revised Edition September 2020

Origination by Pooleys Flight Equipment Limited.

Published by Pooleys Flight Equipment Ltd

Elstree Aerodrome
Hertfordshire WD6 3AW
Tel: +44(0)20 8953 4870
Web: www.pooleys.com
Email: sales@pooleys.com

AUTHOR

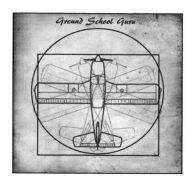

Helena B A Hughes

Helena Hughes was born into an aviation household, having her first informal "flying lesson" at the age of four. Her late father David was a flying instructor and also flew corporate jets. On leaving University Helena obtained her PPL. Shortly afterwards she started work in Air Traffic Control at London Luton Airport earning her Controllers Licence in 1990. Helena continues to be an operational Air Traffic Control Officer and is currently posted to Swanwick working "Thames Radar", "Luton Radar" and "Heathrow Special"; she is involved in controller training as both an Instructor and Assessor. Helena holds a fixed wing CPL/IR and has been a flying instructor since 1996. She also holds a PPL(H) and is a Radio Telephony and Air/Ground Examiner.

Helena would like to thank: Mrs. Brenda "Bedda" Hughes; Mr. Andrew Temple of Solent Flight Ltd; A Vrancken and H Ewing

INTRODUCTION

This book is intended as an aid to revision and examination preparation for those studying for the grant of an EASA PPL. Ideally its use should follow a period of self or directed study to consolidate the knowledge acquired and identify any areas of weakness prior to attempting the PPL examinations themselves.

The questions and answers in this publication are designed to reflect those appearing in the current examination papers and are set out in a representative format. No attempt has been made to replicate any actual examination paper.

Blank answer sheets are provided at the end of the book which may be photocopied to enable multiple attempts at each exam.

EDITORS

Dorothy Saul-Pooley LLB(Hons) FRAeS

Dorothy holds an ATPL (A) and a CPL (H), and is both an instructor and examiner on aeroplanes and an instructor on helicopters. She is Head of Training for a school dedicated to running Flight Instructor courses at Shoreham. She is also a CAA Flight Instructor Examiner. In addition, having qualified as a solicitor in 1982, Dorothy acted for many years as a consultant specialising in aviation and insurance liability issues, and has lectured widely on air law and insurance issues. This highly unusual combination of qualifications led to her appointment as Honorary Solicitor to the Guild of Air Pilots and Navigators (GAPAN). Dorothy is a Fellow of the Royal Aeronautical Society, first Chairman of the GAPAN Instructor Committee, and past Chairman of the Education & Training Committee. She has just completed her term of office as the Master for the year 2014-15 of the Honourable Company of Air Pilots (formerly GAPAN). She is also Chairman of the Professional Flying Instructors Association. In 2003 she was awarded the Jean Lennox Bird Trophy for her contribution to aviation and support of Women in Aviation and the BWPA (British Women Pilots Association). In 2013 Dorothy was awarded the prestigious Master Air Pilots Certificate by GAPAN. A regular contributor to seminars, conferences and aviation publications. Dorothy is the author and editor of a number of flying training books and has published articles in legal and insurance journals.

Daljeet Gill BA(Hons)

Daljeet is the Head of Design & Development for Pooleys Flight Equipment and editor of the Air Pilot's Manuals, Guides to the EASA IR & CPL Flight Test, Pre-flight Briefing and R/T Communications as well as many other publications. Daljeet has been involved with the editing, typesetting and designing of all Pooleys publications and products since she joined us in 2001. Graduating in 1999 with a BA(Hons) in Graphic Design, she deals with marketing, advertising, exhibition design and technical design of our manufactured products in the UK. She maintains our website and produces our Pooleys Catalogue. Daljeet's design skills and imaginative approach have brought a new level of clarity and readability to the projects she has touched.

Sebastian Pooley FRIN FRAeS

Sebastian is Managing Director of Pooleys Flight Equipment and a Director of Air Pilot Publishing. He holds a PPL (A). Sebastian is a Committee Member of the GANG - the General Aviation Navigation Group, part of the Royal Institute of Navigation and a judge for the International Dawn to Dusk Competition. He is a Liveryman of the Honourable Company of Air Pilots, a Fellow of the Royal Institute of Navigation and a Fellow of the Royal Aeronautical Society.

EASA PRIVATE PILOT LICENCE
AEROPLANE & HELICOPTER
HUMAN PERFORMANCE & LIMITATIONS

Before attempting these practice examination papers, you should have read the Air Pilot's Manual, Volume 6 – Human Performance & Limitations and Operational Procedures and have completed the practice questions.

The Human Performance & Limitations examination consists of 12 questions; the time allowed is 25 minutes. Each of the practice examination papers that follow contain 20 questions.

The pass mark is 75%. You must get a minimum of 15 questions correct.

Please read each question carefully and ensure you understand it fully before making your choice of answer.

Each question is multiple choice with four possible answers A, B, C and D.

You should indicate your chosen answer by placing a cross in the appropriate box on the answer sheet.

Blank answer sheets are to be found at the end of this publication, these may be photocopied.

INTENTIONALLY BLANK

HUMAN PERFORMANCE & LIMITATIONS
PAPER 1

1. The Peripheral, Central and Autonomic are what type of system in the body?
   a. Circulatory
   b. Nervous
   c. Cardiac
   d. Digestive

2. The system that moves blood around the body is called the:
   a. Nervous system
   b. Digestive system
   c. Cardiac system
   d. Circulatory system

3. Within the atmosphere the proportion of oxygen:
   a. Increases as altitude increases
   b. Decreases as altitude increases
   c. Remains constant
   d. Initially increases then decreases

4. The body not having sufficient oxygen to meet its requirements is a condition known as:
   a. Hypoxia
   b. Hypoglycemia
   c. Hypochondria
   d. Hyperventilation

5. The initial signs of the onset of hypoxia include:
   a. Dizziness and tingling sensation in the fingers
   b. Euphoria, clumsiness and impaired judgement
   c. Anxiety and tingling sensation in the fingers
   d. Clumsiness and hot flushes

6. Chemical receptors in the brain govern the respiratory process. They are most sensitive to changes in the level of:
   a. Nitrogen
   b. Oxygen
   c. Carbon dioxide
   d. Calcium

7. The "time of useful consciousness" might be defined as:
   a. The time from the onset of hypoxia to unconsciousness
   b. The time from when the air supply is reduced to unconsciousness
   c. The time available to perform useful tasks before hypoxia sets in
   d. The time available before feeling euphoric

8. Although individuals vary, pilots should not suffer the effects of hypoxia when operating up to and including an altitude of:
   a. 8,000 ft
   b. 9,000 ft
   c. 10,000 ft
   d. 12,000 ft

9. The high pressure experienced when scuba diving increases the solubility of nitrogen into the body tissues. Decompression sickness is when:

    a. The muscles start to cramp

    b. The nitrogen forms bubbles when pressure is reduced

    c. The nitrogen forms bubbles when pressure is increased

    d. Dizziness and nausea begin

10. The human auditory range is:

    a. 20 to 20,000 Hz

    b. 20 to 200,000 Hz

    c. 200 to 20,000 Hz

    d. 200 to 200,000 Hz

11. A pilot suffering from gastro-enteritis is:

    a. Probably fit to fly

    b. Fit to fly with medication

    c. Unfit to fly for more than one hour

    d. Unfit to fly

12. With a flight visibility of 3nm a light aircraft and a military jet have a closing speed of 400kts. Approximately how much time do the pilots have to avoid a collision if visual contact was made at maximum range?

    a. Approximately 27 seconds

    b. Approximately 33 seconds

    c. Approximately 38 seconds

    d. Approximately 20 seconds

13. A light aircraft and a military jet are on a head on collision course with a closing speed of around 600 knots. In this situation how would the image of the military jet appear to grow as range decreased?

    a. The image would grow very quickly at a constant rate

    b. Initially the image would show only a small rate of growth until close to impact when it would grow rapidly

    c. Initially it the image would grow rapidly until close to impact when the rate would slow

    d. The image would grow slowly at a constant rate

14. Having allowed sufficient time for night vision to develop, when looking at an object beyond the aircraft, the maximum visual acuity is achieved by looking:

    a. Slightly below the object

    b. 45° to the side of the object

    c. Directly at the object

    d. Slightly off centre by about 10°

15. If a runway is narrower than expected a pilot will tend to:

    a. Fly a lower approach than normal and possibly land short

    b. Fly a lower approach than normal and possibly overshoot

    c. Fly a higher approach than normal and possibly land short

    d. Fly a higher approach than normal and possibly overshoot

16. The way to maintain situational awareness is to:

    a. Fly by reference to the aircraft's instruments

    b. Interpret any new data to confirm where you should be

    c. Maintain heading and obtain continual position fixes

    d. Plan ahead and gather and consider all available data whilst updating your situation.

17. The diagram below represents runways with varying slopes. Which represents a runway with an up slope?

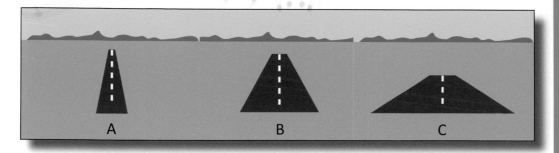

    a.   C
    b.   B
    c.   A
    d.   Between A and B

18. Ideally within a cockpit controls that operate different systems should be designed to:
    a.   Look and feel the same
    b.   Look and feel different
    c.   Look similar and be easy to use
    d.   Look the same but feel different

19. When operating at altitude or above cloud with an empty visual field a pilot should be aware that the eyes will tend to:
    a.   Focus at a point 1 to 2 metres away
    b.   Focus at infinity
    c.   Focus at the horizon
    d.   Focus at a point 10 to 12 metres away

20. The three needle altimeter is considered to be:
    a.   Accurate, reliable and rarely misread
    b.   Accurate, reliable and easily misread
    c.   Reasonably accurate, unreliable but easy to read
    d.   Easily misread by novice pilots

END OF HUMAN PERFORMANCE & LIMITATIONS PAPER 1

	A	B	C	D
1.		X		
2.				X
3.			X	
4.	X			
5.		X		
6.			X	
7.			X	
8.			X	
9.		X		
10.	X			
11.				X
12.	X			
13.		X		
14.				X
15	X			
16.				X
17.			X	
18.		X		
19.	X			
20.		X		

CORRECT ANSWERS: PERCENTAGES					
15	**16**	**17**	**18**	**19**	**20**
75%	80%	85%	90%	95%	100%

HUMAN PERFORMANCE & LIMITATIONS
PAPER 1: EXPLANATIONS

1. **(Answer: B)** The nervous system is composed of the Peripheral, Central and Autonomic systems. The central nervous system is composed of the brain and spinal chord, and is the master controller. The peripheral nervous system, which includes the autonomic system, unconsciously controls body functions such as intestinal movements, heart beat regulation and sweating.

    FURTHER READING: APM VOLUME 6, SECTION 1, CHAPTER 1 – HUMAN PHYSIOLOGY & HIGH ALTITUDES

2. **(Answer: D)** The circulatory, or cardiovascular, system moves blood around the body. It takes oxygen and nutrients to the body tissues and removes waste products and carbon dioxide.

    FURTHER READING: APM VOLUME 6, SECTION 1, CHAPTER 1 – HUMAN PHYSIOLOGY & HIGH ALTITUDES

3. **(Answer: C)** The proportion of the gases which make up the atmosphere remains constant, although the actual mass and number of molecules of each gas is far less at high level. The make up is: Nitrogen 78%, oxygen 21% and small amounts of other gases and water vapour.

    FURTHER READING: APM VOLUME 6, SECTION 1, CHAPTER 1 – HUMAN PHYSIOLOGY & HIGH ALTITUDES

4. **(Answer: A)** A lack of sufficient oxygen to the brain and body is called hypoxia.

    FURTHER READING: APM VOLUME 6, SECTION 1, CHAPTER 1 – HUMAN PHYSIOLOGY & HIGH ALTITUDES

5. **(Answer: B)** Some of the initial symptoms of hypoxia include a sense of euphoria or well-being, impaired judgement, a difficulty completing mental tasks and a loss of muscle control.

SYMPTOMS OF HYPOXIA – initial signs first
Personality changes (euphoria) and impaired judgement
Confusion and difficulty concentrating
Loss of co-ordination (clumsiness)
Drowsiness
Headache, dizziness and nausea
Blue tinge to skin
Hyperventilation
Loss of basic senses – vision is likely to be first
Unconsciousness

    FURTHER READING: APM VOLUME 6, SECTION 1, CHAPTER 1 – HUMAN PHYSIOLOGY & HIGH ALTITUDES

6. **(Answer: C)** Receptors in the brain are most sensitive to any changes in the level carbon dioxide; such changes in the level of carbon dioxide will trigger either an increase or decrease in breathing rate.

    FURTHER READING: APM VOLUME 6, SECTION 1, CHAPTER 1 – HUMAN PHYSIOLOGY & HIGH ALTITUDES

7. **(Answer: C)** The time of useful consciousness may be described as the time available to pilots to perform useful tasks, without using supplemental oxygen, before hypoxia sets in and compromises their ability to deal with the situation. The symptoms of hypoxia are likely to begin above 10,000 feet (lower in some individuals, especially smokers); its effects are accelerated at higher altitudes where lower partial pressures of oxygen exist.

ALTITUDE TIME OF USEFUL CONSCIOUSNESS	
20,000 ft AMSL	5 to 10 minutes
30,0000 ft AMSL	45 to 75 seconds
40,000 ft AMSL	18 to 30 seconds
45,000 ft AMSL	12 seconds

FURTHER READING: APM VOLUME 6, SECTION 1, CHAPTER 1 – HUMAN PHYSIOLOGY & HIGH ALTITUDES

8. **(Answer: C)** Above 8,000 ft the effects of oxygen deprivation may start to be evident, especially in pilots under stress. At a cabin altitude of 10,000 ft most people can still deal with the reduced oxygen supply for short periods. Flight above 10,000 ft should not be prolonged without the use of supplemental oxygen.

FURTHER READING: APM VOLUME 6, SECTION 1, CHAPTER 1 – HUMAN PHYSIOLOGY & HIGH ALTITUDES

9. **(Answer: B)** The use of compressed air when scuba diving has been known to lead to decompression sickness (the bends) during flight as low as 6,000 feet. At high pressures nitrogen is absorbed into the blood. When pressure is reduced bubbles of nitrogen form in the bloodstream causing pain and immobility in the joints.

FURTHER READING: APM VOLUME 6, SECTION 1, CHAPTER 1 – HUMAN PHYSIOLOGY & HIGH ALTITUDES

10. **(Answer: A)** Human hearing is in the range of 20 Hz to 20,000 Hz. Voices are between 500 Hz and 3,000 Hz.

FURTHER READING: APM VOLUME 6, SECTION 1, CHAPTER 3 – HEARING AND BALANCE

11. **(Answer: D)** Gastro-enteritis can be extremely debilitating even with medication. It is an inflammation of the stomach and intestines often causing sudden and violent bouts of diarrhoea and vomiting. A pilot with gastro-enteritis will be unfit to fly.

FURTHER READING: APM VOLUME 6, SECTION 1, CHAPTER 4 – AM I FIT TO FLY?

12. **(Answer: A)** Visibility 3 nm and closing speed 400 knots.

Time = $\dfrac{Distance}{Speed}$

Time = 3/400 = 0.0075 hours

This is the answer in hours. To obtain the seconds we must multiply by 60 twice (once to get an answer in minutes and again to get seconds).

0.0075 x 60 = 0.45 minutes
0.45 x 60 = 27 seconds.
Nearest answer 27 seconds

FURTHER READING: APM VOLUME 6, SECTION 1, CHAPTER 2 – EYESIGHT & VISUAL ILLUSIONS

13. **(Answer: B)** The image of an aircraft approaching head-on at high speed would remain small, growing only slowly until it is very close. It will then appear to grow very quickly.

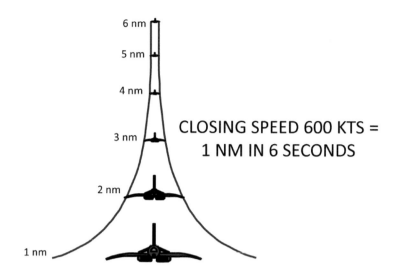

CLOSING SPEED 600 KTS =
1 NM IN 6 SECONDS

6 nm
5 nm
4 nm
3 nm
2 nm
1 nm

FURTHER READING: APM VOLUME 6, SECTION 1, CHAPTER 2 – EYESIGHT & VISUAL ILLUSIONS

14. **(Answer: D)** An object at night will be more readily visible when looking to the side of it by 10 to 20°, rather than directly at it. It is more effective at night to scan more slowly to permit such "off-centre" viewing of objects in your peripheral vision.

FURTHER READING: APM VOLUME 6, SECTION 1, CHAPTER 2 – EYESIGHT & VISUAL ILLUSIONS

15. **(Answer: A)** A narrow runway will create the illusion of being too high, meaning you fly lower than "normal" with the possibility of undershooting the runway threshold or landing earlier (and probably more heavily) than expected.

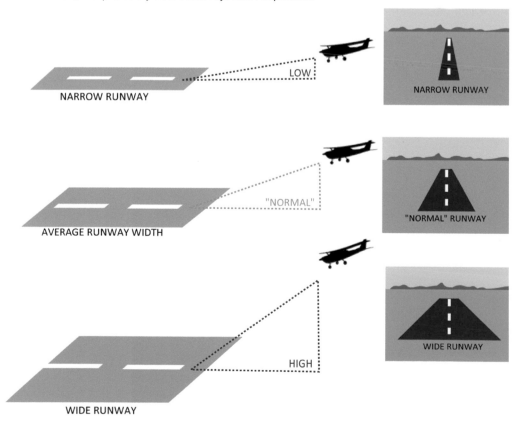

LOW
NARROW RUNWAY
NARROW RUNWAY

"NORMAL"
AVERAGE RUNWAY WIDTH
"NORMAL" RUNWAY

HIGH
WIDE RUNWAY
WIDE RUNWAY

FURTHER READING: APM VOLUME 6, SECTION 1, CHAPTER 2 – EYESIGHT & VISUAL ILLUSIONS

16. **(Answer: D)** In a pilot situational awareness means maintaining an accurate mental model of the environment. This requires that all available data is gathered, considered and interpreted. The situation should be regularly updated and good forward planning employed. It is an on-going process of observation and analysis of the information available to maintain an accurate mental model.

FURTHER READING: APM VOLUME 6, SECTION 1, CHAPTER 8 – AIRMANSHIP & THREAT AND ERROR MANAGEMENT

17. **(Answer: C)** An up sloping runway will look longer than it really is. "C" is the perspective for a down sloping runway, "B" for a level runway and "A" represents an up slope.

UPSLOPE   LEVEL GROUND   DOWNSLOPE

FURTHER READING: APM VOLUME 6, SECTION 1, CHAPTER 2 – EYESIGHT & VISUAL ILLUSIONS

18. **(Answer: B)** As an aid to preventing incorrect selection, differentiation should be built into the design of controls enabling the pilot to easily identify the control by its shape, colour and feel. In particular colocated controls should be made to look and feel different.

FURTHER READING: APM VOLUME 6, SECTION 1, CHAPTER 9 – THE FLIGHT DECK

19. **(Answer: A)** It may be difficult to detect other aircraft when there is an empty field of vision as the eyes have a natural resting tendency to focus at 1 to 2 metres. This is called "empty field myopia" and can be avoided by focusing on any available distant object to lengthen the focus, (e.g. a landmark or cloud), or if none are available a relatively distant part of the aircraft.

FURTHER READING: APM VOLUME 6, SECTION 1, CHAPTER 2 – EYESIGHT & VISUAL ILLUSIONS

20. **(Answer: B)** A three point altimeter takes longer to read. Although it is very accurate it can be easily misinterpreted.

FURTHER READING: APM VOLUME 6, SECTION 1, CHAPTER 9 – THE FLIGHT DECK

END OF EXPLANATIONS PAPER 1

HUMAN PERFORMANCE & LIMITATIONS
PAPER 2

1. The function of the circulatory system is to:

   a. Supply energy to the cells
   b. Remove the products of digestion
   c. Supply oxygen and nutrients to the body cells and remove waste products
   d. Supply carbon dioxide and nutrients to the body cells and remove waste

2. There are three nervous systems within the body. These are:

   a. Peripheral, Core and Automatic
   b. Peripheral, Core and Autonomic
   c. Peripheral, Central and Autonomic
   d. Peripheral, Central and Automatic

3. Respiration takes place as an involuntary action. It is regulated by:

   a. The amount of oxygen in the blood
   b. Any changes in air pressure
   c. Any changes in altitude
   d. The amount of carbon dioxide in the blood

4. Compared with a non-smoker, a tobacco smoker is likely to experience the symptoms of hypoxia at:

   a. A lower cabin altitude
   b. A higher cabin altitude
   c. The same cabin altitude
   d. Any altitude

5. Hyperventilation may be brought on by lack of oxygen, other possible causes are:

   a. Dehydration
   b. Concentrating too hard on a complex task
   c. Exhaustion
   d. Anxiety, heat, motion sickness or vibration

6. After scuba diving pilots are advised not to fly within ...(i)... hours, or ...(ii)... hours if a depth of 30 feet has been exceeded:

   a. i) 8   ii) 16
   b. i) 12   ii) 24
   c. i) 16   ii) 32
   d. i) 24   ii) 48

7. Decompression sickness is caused when which gas comes out of solution to form bubbles in the body tissues?

   a. Hydrogen
   b. Oxygen
   c. Nitrogen
   d. Carbon dioxide

8. Sensations of dizziness, tingling fingers and lips and anxiety experienced whilst operating below 10,000 ft AMSL, would indicate:

   a. Hypoxia
   b. Hyperglycemia
   c. Hyperactivity
   d. Hyperventilation

9.   A remedy for hyperventilation is:

   a.   Consciously slowing down the rate of breathing
   b.   Giving oxygen
   c.   A good slap
   d.   Consciously speeding up the rate of breathing

10.   How might carbon monoxide enter the cockpit?

   a.   A leak in the oxygen system
   b.   A leak in the cockpit heater or cigarette smoke
   c.   Passenger's breath
   d.   A cracked windscreen

11.   Assume one unit is half a pint of beer, a standard glass of wine or a single measure of spirit. Approximately how long will it take to eliminate one unit of alcohol from the blood?

   a.   1 hour
   b.   30 minutes
   c.   2 hours
   d.   3 hours

12.   Full adaptation to night vision in normal conditions takes:

   a.   15 to 20 minutes
   b.   10 to 15 minutes
   c.   30 to 40 minutes
   d.   40 to 45 minutes

13.   The Eustachian tube serves what purpose?

   a.   It allows the middle ear to drain
   b.   It allows pressure in the middle ear to equalise with ambient pressure
   c.   It allows pressure in the outer ear to equalise with ambient pressure
   d.   It allows pressure in the sinus to equalise with middle ear pressure

14.   With a flight visibility of 3nm a light aircraft and a military jet have a closing speed of 360kts. Approximately how much time do the pilots have to avoid a collision if visual contact was made at maximum range?

   a.   Approximately 20 seconds
   b.   Approximately 25 seconds
   c.   Approximately 30 seconds
   d.   Approximately 40 seconds

15.   The visibility is 5 km, a military aircraft is operating at a speed of 420 knots; a light aircraft is approaching head on at a speed of 120 knots. The pilots will have a maximum time of .... in which to see the other aircraft and take avoiding action. Complete the statement.

   a.   Approximately 40 seconds
   b.   Approximately 35 seconds
   c.   Approximately 30 seconds
   d.   Approximately 20 seconds

16.   The most effective method of visual scanning is:

   a.   A series of short regularly spaced eye movements to search 10° sector of sky
   b.   Slowly sweep the entire field of view from left to right
   c.   Concentrate on the most likely areas for traffic
   d.   Quickly sweep the entire field of view from left to right

17. A pilot in straight and level flight but decelerating may experience the illusory perception of:

   a. Rolling left

   b. Yawing right

   c. Pitching down

   d. Pitching up

18. Flying a visual approach to a down sloping runway which lacks any visual glide slope aids, is likely to result in a:

   a. Shallower approach than intended

   b. Close to the intended flight path

   c. Steeper approach than intended

   d. Very erratic approach

19. The best method of maintaining situational awareness is to:

   a. Consider all available data whilst updating your situation and planning ahead

   b. Ignore information that does not agree with your mental model

   c. Rely on experience

   d. Concentrate on where you are going

20. A pilot intending to self-medicate using a preparation that does not require a doctor's prescription should:

   a. Check that the side effects have been evaluated and are minor

   b. See if the drugs have any side effects before flying

   c. Seek professional advice from a CAA AME

   d. Be aware of any likely performance reducing side effects

---

END OF HUMAN PERFORMANCE & LIMITATIONS PAPER 2

	A	B	C	D
1.			X	
2.			X	
3.				X
4.	X			
5.				X
6.		X		
7.			X	
8.				X
9.	X			
10.		X		
11.	X			
12.			X	
13.		X		
14.			X	
15				X
16.	X			
17.			X	
18.			X	
19.	X			
20.			X	

CORRECT ANSWERS: PERCENTAGES					
15	16	17	18	19	20
75%	80%	85%	90%	95%	100%

HUMAN PERFORMANCE & LIMITATIONS
PAPER 2: EXPLANATIONS

1. **(Answer: C)** The circulatory, or cardiovascular, system moves blood around the body. It takes oxygen and nutrients to the body tissues and removes waste products and carbon dioxide.

   FURTHER READING: APM VOLUME 6, SECTION 1, CHAPTER 1 – HUMAN PHYSIOLOGY & HIGH ALTITUDES

2. **(Answer: C)** The nervous system is composed of the Peripheral, Central and Autonomic systems. The central nervous system is composed of the brain and spinal chord and is the master controller. The peripheral nervous system, which includes the autonomic system, unconsciously controls body functions such as intestinal movements, heart beat regulation and sweating.

   FURTHER READING: APM VOLUME 6, SECTION 1, CHAPTER 1 – HUMAN PHYSIOLOGY & HIGH ALTITUDES

3. **(Answer: D)** Receptors in the brain are very sensitive to any changes in carbon dioxide; changes in the level of carbon dioxide will trigger either an increase or decrease in breathing rate.

   FURTHER READING: APM VOLUME 6, SECTION 1, CHAPTER 1 – HUMAN PHYSIOLOGY & HIGH ALTITUDES

4. **(Answer: A)** Haemoglobin is a blood protein in red blood cells which combines with oxygen to transport it around the body. Haemoglobin has a higher affinity for carbon monoxide than it does for oxygen. The excess carbon monoxide in tobacco smoke will reduce the amount of oxygen in the blood stream, meaning that the symptoms of hypoxia could manifest at lower altitude.

   FURTHER READING: APM VOLUME 6, SECTION 1, CHAPTER 1 – HUMAN PHYSIOLOGY & HIGH ALTITUDES

5. **(Answer: D)** Hyperventilation is a condition where breathing is more rapid and deeper than is necessary; resulting in too much carbon dioxide being flushed from the body upsetting its chemical balance. Hyperventilation is most often associated with anxiety or intense stress; but may also be caused by vibration, turbulence, motion sickness and is itself a symptom of hypoxia.

   FURTHER READING: APM VOLUME 6, SECTION 1, CHAPTER 1 – HUMAN PHYSIOLOGY & HIGH ALTITUDES

6. **(Answer: B)** The use of compressed air when scuba diving has been known to lead to decompression sickness (the bends) during flight as low as 6,000 feet. At high pressures nitrogen is absorbed into the blood, when pressure is reduced bubbles of nitrogen form in the body tissues; causing pain and immobility in the joints. You should not fly within 12 hours of any scuba dive using compressed air and within 24 hours if a depth of 30 feet has been exceeded.

   FURTHER READING: APM VOLUME 6, SECTION 1, CHAPTER 1 – HUMAN PHYSIOLOGY & HIGH ALTITUDES

7. **(Answer: C)** The use of compressed air when scuba diving has been known to lead to decompression sickness (the bends) during flight as low as 6,000 feet. At high pressures nitrogen is absorbed into the blood, when pressure is reduced bubbles of nitrogen form in the bloodstream causing pain and immobility in the joints.

   FURTHER READING: APM VOLUME 6, SECTION 1, CHAPTER 1 – HUMAN PHYSIOLOGY & HIGH ALTITUDES

8.   **(Answer: D)** Below 10,000 ft these symptoms would indicate hyperventilation. Hyperventilation is a condition where breathing is more rapid and deeper than is necessary; resulting in too much carbon dioxide being flushed from the body upsetting its chemical balance. Hyperventilation is most often associated with anxiety or intense stress; but may also be caused by vibration, turbulence, motion sickness and is itself a symptom of hypoxia.

SYMPTOMS OF HYPERVENTILATION
Dizziness, light headedness
Tingling sensations – especially in fingers, hands, lips and feet
Visual impairment – blurring, clouded or tunnel vision
Hot and cold feelings
Unconsciousness

FURTHER READING: APM VOLUME 6, SECTION 1, CHAPTER 1 – HUMAN PHYSIOLOGY & HIGH ALTITUDES

9.   **(Answer: A)** Remedies for hyperventilation: Consciously slowing down the breathing rate (talking helps) Breathing in and out of a paper bag (increases carbon dioxide level in the blood) If no recovery is evident, suspect hypoxia instead.

FURTHER READING: APM VOLUME 6, SECTION 1, CHAPTER 1 – HUMAN PHYSIOLOGY & HIGH ALTITUDES

10.   **(Answer: B)** Carbon monoxide is present in cigarette smoke. Light aircraft cabin heaters are often heat exchangers from a shroud around the engine exhaust system; alternatively a combustion heater may be fitted. As carbon monoxide is present in exhaust fumes a leak in either type of heat exchanger could lead to carbon monoxide mixing with the fresh heated air and being channelled into the cockpit.

FURTHER READING: APM VOLUME 6, SECTION 1, CHAPTER 1 – HUMAN PHYSIOLOGY & HIGH ALTITUDES

11.   **(Answer: A)** It takes the liver approximately one hour to remove one unit of alcohol from the blood stream.

FURTHER READING: APM VOLUME 6, SECTION 1, CHAPTER 4 – AM I FIT TO FLY?

12.   **(Answer: C)** The rods are most important for night vision and take around 30 minutes to adapt to darkness. Bright lights will immediately impair your night vision adaptation and should be avoided in the 30 minutes prior to night flight.

FURTHER READING: APM VOLUME 6, SECTION 1, CHAPTER 2 – EYESIGHT & VISUAL ILLUSIONS

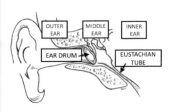

13.   **(Answer: B)** The Eustachian tube enables pressure in the middle ear to be maintained at the same value as ambient pressure. It connects the interior of the middle ear with the nasal passages.

FURTHER READING: APM VOLUME 6, SECTION 1, CHAPTER 3 – HEARING & BALANCE

14.   **(Answer: C)** Visibility 3 nm and closing speed 360 knots.

Time = $\dfrac{\text{Distance}}{\text{Speed}}$

Time =   3/360   =   0.00834 hours

This is the answer in hours. To obtain the seconds we must multiply by 60 twice (once to get an answer in minutes and again to get seconds).

0.00834 x 60 = 0.5004 minutes
0.5004 x 60 = 30.024 seconds.
Nearest answer 30 seconds

FURTHER READING: APM VOLUME 6, SECTION 1, CHAPTER 2 – EYESIGHT & VISUAL ILLUSIONS

15. **(Answer: D)** Visibility 5 km and closing speed 540 knots.

5 km = roughly 2.7 nm
Time = $\dfrac{\text{Distance}}{\text{Speed}}$

Time = 2.7/540 = 0.005 hours

This is the answer in hours. To obtain the seconds we must multiply by 60 twice (once to get an answer in minutes and again to get seconds).

0.005 x 60 = 0.3 minutes
0.3 x 60 = 18 seconds.
Nearest answer 20 seconds

FURTHER READING: APM VOLUME 6, SECTION 1, CHAPTER 2 – EYESIGHT & VISUAL ILLUSIONS

16. **(Answer: A)** The most effective method of scanning for other aircraft during the day is to use a series of short, regularly spaced eye movements to search each 10° sector of the sky.

FURTHER READING: APM VOLUME 6, SECTION 1, CHAPTER 2 – EYESIGHT & VISUAL ILLUSIONS

17. **(Answer: C)** In an aircraft flying straight and level at constant speed gravity acts straight down. If the aircraft decelerates an extra force - inertia - is added and sensed by the otoliths in the inner ear. During deceleration the resultant force between "real up" and inertia due to the speed change is perceived as "up" leading to the sensation that the aircraft has pitched down. Therefore deceleration is sensed as a false pitch down; the danger being that the pilot will react by pitching up to correct leading to the speed decaying and a further temptation to pitch up.

During a rapid deceleration the body senses the rearward angled resultant force as "up" causing the pilot to feel as if the aircraft has pitched down.

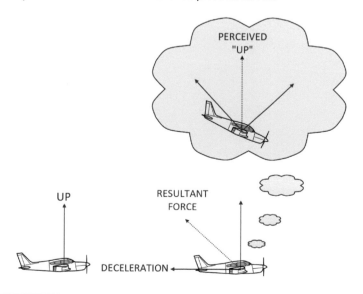

FURTHER READING: APM VOLUME 6, SECTION 1, CHAPTER 3 – HEARING & BALANCE

18. **(Answer: C)** A down sloping runway will look shorter than it really is, hence the pilot will feel low on the approach. The tendency will be to fly higher and make a steeper approach.

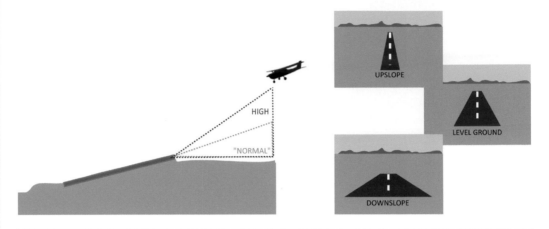

FURTHER READING: APM VOLUME 6, SECTION 1, CHAPTER 2 – EYESIGHT & VISUAL ILLUSIONS

19. **(Answer: A)** In a pilot situational awareness means maintaining an accurate mental model of the environment. This requires that all available data is gathered, considered and interpreted. The situation should be regularly updated and good forward planning employed. It is an on-going process of observation and analysis of the information available to maintain an accurate mental model.

FURTHER READING: APM VOLUME 6, SECTION 1, CHAPTER 8 – AIRMANSHIP & THREAT AND ERROR MANAAGEMENT

20. **(Answer: C)** It is advisable not to take any medicines before or during flight. If any doubt exists as to a non-prescription drug's effect an aviation doctor should be consulted.

FURTHER READING: APM VOLUME 6, SECTION 1, CHAPTER 4 – AM I FIT TO FLY?

END OF EXPLANATIONS PAPER 2

HUMAN PERFORMANCE & LIMITATIONS
PAPER 3

1. As altitude increases the oxygen available to the body reduces because of a:

    a. Decrease in temperature
    b. Decrease in pressure
    c. Decrease in the proportion of oxygen
    d. Decrease in the proportion of carbon dioxide

2. Haemoglobin, a protein in red blood cells, transports oxygen but will more readily combine with:

    a. Nitrogen
    b. Carbon dioxide
    c. Hydrogen
    d. Carbon monoxide

3. Hyperventilation may be remedied by:

    a. Increasing the breathing rate
    b. Applying a cold compress
    c. Breathing in and out of a paper bag
    d. Shocking the subject

4. After scuba diving to depths in excess of 30 feet, you should allow:

    a. 6 hours before flying
    b. 12 hours before flying
    c. 24 hours before flying
    d. 48 hours before flying

5. The part of the eye that is sensitive to light is called the:

    a. Iris
    b. Lens
    c. Fovea
    d. Retina

6. Why should you not fly when suffering from a cold?

    a. The pressure between the inner ear and the middle ear may not be equalised
    b. The pressure between the inner ear and atmospheric air may not be equalised
    c. The pressure between the middle ear and atmospheric may not be equalised
    d. The pressure between the middle ear and the outer ear may not be equalised

7. With a flight visibility of 5 nm a light aircraft and a military jet have a closing speed of 500 knots. Approximately how much time do the pilots have to avoid a collision if visual contact was made at maximum range?

    a. 50 to 60 seconds
    b. 40 to 50 seconds
    c. 30 to 40 seconds
    d. 20 to 30 seconds

8. A light aircraft and a military jet have a closing speed of 500 knots. The visibility is 5 nm; however the pilots do not see each other's aircraft until there is 3 nm between them. How much time would the pilots have to avoid a collision?

    a. Approximately 30 seconds
    b. Approximately 20 seconds
    c. Approximately 40 seconds
    d. Approximately 50 seconds

9. In an aircraft with a design eye position indication seating should be:

    a.   Adjusted during the cruise to allow the pilot optimum scan position

    b.   Adjusted for take-off and landing

    c.   Left as it was found, the previous pilot will have adjusted it

    d.   Adjusted prior to departure and used for all phases of flight

10. A pilot can be said to be .....(?)..... when his/her perception of where he/she thinks the aircraft is matches where the aircraft actually is.

    a.   Lucky

    b.   Situationally aware

    c.   On track

    d.   On flight plan

11. Flying a visual approach to an up sloping runway which lacks any visual glide slope aids, is likely to result in:

    a.   A shallower approach than intended

    b.   An approach close to the intended flight path

    c.   A steeper approach than intended

    d.   A very erratic approach

12. If a runway is wider than expected a pilot will tend to:

    a.   Fly a lower approach than normal and possibly land short

    b.   Fly a lower approach than normal and possibly overshoot

    c.   Fly a higher approach than normal and possibly land short

    d.   Fly a higher approach than normal and possibly overshoot

13. A pilot in straight and level flight but accelerating may experience the illusory perception of:

    a.   Pitching up

    b.   Pitching down

    c.   Rolling right

    d.   Yawing left

14. Flying in hazy conditions may lead a pilot to believe that objects outside the aircraft are:

    a.   Closer than in reality

    b.   Further away than they are

    c.   Larger than they actually are

    d.   Closer and smaller than in reality

15. During a flight a pilot experienced prolonged exposure to exhaust gases, when could he/she be considered fit to fly again?

    a.   After one or two hours

    b.   After 4 or 5 hours

    c.   After several days

    d.   After 24 hours

16. One cause of motion sickness is:

    a.   The movement of fluid in the inner ear

    b.   Too many visual clues

    c.   Eating shortly before flight

    d.   A mismatch between signals from the eyes and the inner ear

17. Pilots who are aware they are experiencing spatial disorientation should:

    a. Briefly close their eyes
    b. Concentrate on and trust the aircraft instruments
    c. Rely on external visual clues
    d. Rely on somatosensory (seat of the pants) information

18. A prominent sloping cloud layer across your flight path may lead you to:

    a. Pitch up
    b. Bank the aircraft
    c. Apply more rudder
    d. Descend

19. Imagine you are flying with a more experienced pilot; he has chosen a course of action which you believe may endanger the flight. What should you do?

    a. Accept the course of action so as not to compromise your relationship
    b. Question his judgement only if you think he will react positively
    c. Always express any doubts
    d. Accept the course of action but be prepared to take control

20. When operating at low level a person breathing abnormally and displaying the symptoms of hypoxia is probably suffering from:

    a. Hypoxia
    b. Motion sickness
    c. Fear of flying
    d. Hyperventilation

END OF HUMAN PERFORMANCE & LIMITATIONS PAPER 3

HUMAN PERFORMANCE & LIMITATIONS
PAPER 3: ANSWERS

	A	B	C	D
1.		X		
2.				X
3.			X	
4.			X	
5.				X
6.			X	
7.			X	
8.		X		
9.				X
10.		X		
11.	X			
12.				X
13.	X			
14.		X		
15			X	
16.				X
17.		X		
18.		X		
19.			X	
20.				X

CORRECT ANSWERS: PERCENTAGES					
15	16	17	18	19	20
75%	80%	85%	90%	95%	100%

HUMAN PERFORMANCE & LIMITATIONS
PAPER 3: EXPLANATIONS

1. **(Answer: B)** Air pressure reduces with altitude, as does the partial pressure of each constituent gas. The total air pressure being the sum of all the partial pressures. When air pressure falls so does the partial pressure of oxygen, meaning less oxygen is transferred into the bloodstream from the lungs.

   FURTHER READING: APM VOLUME 6, SECTION 1, CHAPTER 1 – HUMAN PHYSIOLOGY & HIGH ALTITUDES

2. **(Answer: D)** Haemoglobin is a blood protein in red blood cells which combines with oxygen to transport it around the body. Haemoglobin has a higher affinity for carbon monoxide than it does for oxygen.

   FURTHER READING: APM VOLUME 6, SECTION 1, CHAPTER 1 – HUMAN PHYSIOLOGY & HIGH ALTITUDES

3. **(Answer: C)** Remedies for hyperventilation: Consciously slowing down the breathing rate (talking helps) Breathing in and out of a paper bag (increases carbon dioxide level in the blood) If no recovery is evident, suspect hypoxia instead.

   FURTHER READING: APM VOLUME 6, SECTION 1, CHAPTER 1 – HUMAN PHYSIOLOGY & HIGH ALTITUDES

4. **(Answer: C)** The use of compressed air when scuba diving has been known to lead to decompression sickness (the bends) during flight as low as 6,000 feet. At high pressures nitrogen is absorbed into the blood. When pressure is reduced bubbles of nitrogen form in the body tissues; causing pain and immobility in the joints. You should not fly within 12 hours of any scuba dive using compressed air, and within 24 hours if a depth of 30 feet has been exceeded.

   FURTHER READING: APM VOLUME 6, SECTION 1, CHAPTER 1 – HUMAN PHYSIOLOGY & HIGH ALTITUDES

5. **(Answer: D)** The retina is the light sensitive layer at the back of the eye. It contains two types of light sensitive cells: rods (black and white) and cones (colour and fine detail).

   FURTHER READING: APM VOLUME 6, SECTION 1, CHAPTER 2 – EYESIGHT & VISUAL ILLUSIONS

6. **(Answer: C)** The Eustachian tube enables pressure in the middle ear to be maintained at the same value as ambient pressure. It connects the interior of the middle ear with the nasal passages. When a person has a cold the Eustachian tubes become swollen and inflamed hindering passage of air. The subsequent pressure equalisation problems, especially during descent, not only lead to pain, but also there is a danger of the eardrum collapsing inward meaning possible permanent hearing loss.

   FURTHER READING: APM VOLUME 6, SECTION 1, CHAPTER 3 – HEARING & BALANCE

7. **(Answer: C)** Visibility 5 nm and closing speed 500 knots.

   Time = Distance
   ⠀⠀⠀⠀⠀⠀⠀⠀Speed
   Time = 5/500 = 0.1 hours

   This is the answer in hours. To obtain the seconds we must multiply by 60 twice (once to get an answer in minutes and again to get seconds).

   0.1 x 60 = 0.6 minutes
   0.45 x 60 = 36 seconds.
   Nearest answer 30 to 40 seconds

   FURTHER READING: APM VOLUME 6, SECTION 1, CHAPTER 2 – EYESIGHT & VISUAL ILLUSIONS

8.   **(Answer: B)** Visibility 3 nm and closing speed 500 knots.

Time = Distance
                    Speed

Time = 3/500 = 0.006 hours

This is the answer in hours. To obtain the seconds we must multiply by 60 twice (once to get an answer in minutes and again to get seconds).

0.006 x 60 = 0.36 minutes
60   = 21.6 seconds.
Nearest answer 20 seconds

FURTHER READING: APM VOLUME 6, SECTION 1, CHAPTER 2 – EYESIGHT & VISUAL ILLUSIONS

---

9.   **(Answer: D)** The desired seating position should be adjusted before departure and used for all phases of flight. The seat should be comfortable and in a position that allows full control movement as well as permitting a balance between a full instrument scan and good outside visibility to be achieved.

FURTHER READING: APM VOLUME 6, SECTION 1, CHAPTER 9 – THE FLIGHT DECK

---

10.   **(Answer: B)** In a pilot situational awareness means maintaining an accurate mental model of the environment. This requires that all available data is gathered, considered and interpreted. The situation should be regularly updated and good forward planning employed. It is an ongoing process of observation and analysis of the information available to maintain an accurate mental model.

FURTHER READING: APM VOLUME 6, SECTION 1, CHAPTER 8 – AIRMANSHIP & THREAT AND ERROR MANAGEMENT

---

11.   **(Answer: A)** An up sloping runway will look longer than it really is, hence the pilot will feel high on the approach. The tendency will be to fly lower and make a shallower approach.

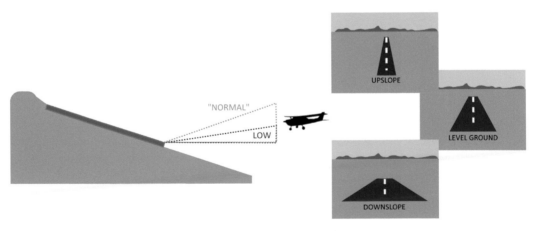

FURTHER READING: APM VOLUME 6, SECTION 1, CHAPTER 2 – EYESIGHT & VISUAL ILLUSIONS

---

12. (Answer: D) A wide runway will create the illusion of being too low. This can lead to flying the approach higher than "normal" and overshooting the threshold. In the latter stages you may also flare and hold off too high.

NARROW RUNWAY   "NORMAL" RUNWAY   WIDE RUNWAY

FURTHER READING: APM VOLUME 6, SECTION 1, CHAPTER 2 – EYESIGHT & VISUAL ILLUSIONS

13. (Answer: A) In an aircraft flying straight and level at constant speed gravity acts straight down. If the aircraft decelerates an extra force - inertia – is added and sensed by the otoliths in the inner ear. Acceleration is sensed as a false pitch up; the tendency being that the pilot will want to pitch the aircraft's nose down.

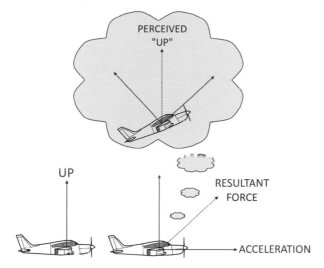

FURTHER READING: APM VOLUME 6, SECTION 1, CHAPTER 3 – HEARING & BALANCE

14. (Answer: B) In hazy conditions depth perception can be difficult; the light rays are refracted, reducing their resolution and colours are muted. This leads to the illusion that objects are further away than they actually are, i.e. you are closer to them than you think.

FURTHER READING: APM VOLUME 6, SECTION 1, CHAPTER 2 – EYESIGHT & VISUAL ILLUSIONS

15. (Answer: C) Haemoglobin is a blood protein in red blood cells which combines with oxygen to transport it around the body. Haemoglobin has a higher affinity for carbon monoxide than it does for oxygen. Carbon monoxide is especially dangerous as it is colourless, odourless and has no taste. Recovery from prolonged exposure may take several days, even on pure oxygen.

FURTHER READING: APM VOLUME 6, SECTION 1, CHAPTER 1 – HUMAN PHYSIOLOGY & HIGH ALTITUDES

16. (Answer: D) Motion sickness can be caused by a mismatch of signals from the balance mechanism in the inner ears and visual signals from the eyes.

FURTHER READING: APM VOLUME 6, SECTION 1, CHAPTER 3 – HEARING & BALANCE

17. **(Answer: B)** Orientation is our ability to determine our position in space. It is normally achieved using a combination of vision, balance and somatosensory (bodily feel or "seat of the pants") information. In most situations theses three inputs reinforce each other; this is not always so in flight. Sometimes the brain can misinterpret some of the information leading to spatial disorientation (not knowing which way is up). We should concentrate on and trust the aircraft instruments.

FURTHER READING: APM VOLUME 6, SECTION 1, CHAPTER 3 – HEARING & BALANCE

18. **(Answer: B)** A very prominent sloping cloud layer may obscure the natural horizon, either partially or totally, creating the illusion that the aircraft is in a banked attitude. If this is believed the reaction would be to fly the aircraft in a banked attitude with cross controls to maintain heading.

FURTHER READING: APM VOLUME 6, SECTION 1, CHAPTER 2 – EYESIGHT & VISUAL ILLUSIONS

19. **(Answer: C)** Any pilot irrespective of experience or status should express any doubts relating to the actions of a more experienced pilot if such actions are perceived as dangerous or inappropriate. Do not be intimidated – experience does not stop a person being fallible!

FURTHER READING: APM VOLUME 6, SECTION 1, CHAPTER 7 – JUDGEMENT & DECISION-MAKING

20. **(Answer: D)** Abnormal breathing is a sign of both hypoxia and hyperventilation. Hypoxia is rare below 10,000 feet. At low level a person breathing abnormally is probably hyperventilating.

SYMPTOMS OF HYPOXIA – initial signs first
Personality changes (euphoria) and impaired judgement
Confusion and difficulty concentrating
Loss of co-ordination (clumsiness)
Drowsiness
Headache, dizziness and nausea
Blue tinge to skin
Hyperventilation
Loss of basic senses – vision is likely to be first
Unconsciousness

SYMPTOMS OF HYPERVENTILATION
Dizziness, light headedness
Tingling sensations – especially in fingers, hands, lips and feet
Visual impairment – blurring, clouded or tunnel vision
Hot and cold feelings
Unconsciousness

FURTHER READING: APM VOLUME 6, SECTION 1, CHAPTER 1 – HUMAN PHYSIOLOGY & HIGH ALTITUDES

END OF EXPLANATIONS PAPER 3

Additional Blank Answer Sheets

INTENTIONALLY BLANK

ANSWER SHEETS

PAPER NO.				
	A	B	C	D
1				
2				
3				
4				
5				
6				
7				
8				
9				
10				
11				
12				
13				
14				
15				
16				
17				
18				
19				
20				

PAPER NO.				
	A	B	C	D
1				
2				
3				
4				
5				
6				
7				
8				
9				
10				
11				
12				
13				
14				
15				
16				
17				
18				
19				
20				

PAPER NO.				
	A	B	C	D
1				
2				
3				
4				
5				
6				
7				
8				
9				
10				
11				
12				
13				
14				
15				
16				
17				
18				
19				
20				

PAPER NO.				
	A	B	C	D
1				
2				
3				
4				
5				
6				
7				
8				
9				
10				
11				
12				
13				
14				
15				
16				
17				
18				
19				
20				

PAPER NO.				
	A	B	C	D
1				
2				
3				
4				
5				
6				
7				
8				
9				
10				
11				
12				
13				
14				
15				
16				
17				
18				
19				
20				

PAPER NO.				
	A	B	C	D
1				
2				
3				
4				
5				
6				
7				
8				
9				
10				
11				
12				
13				
14				
15				
16				
17				
18				
19				
20				